HYSTERICAL HISTORIES

VIRGINIA HALLAM FINDLOW

HYSTERICAL HISTORIES

Windy Row Press

PUBLISHERS

Peterborough, New Hampshire

Printed in the United States of America

FOR ALL MY DEAR ONES

JUST FOR FUN AND
TO STIMULATE FURTHER
INVESTIGATION

HYSTERICAL HISTORIES

ACHILLES, GREEK LEGEND,
HERO OF THE ILIAD,
A FOREMOST WARRIOR
IN THE
TROJAN WAR

Half a human, half divine,
Achilles was a rare combine.
At Troy a hero, Hector's doom,
He thought he'd never need a tomb:
His ma had dipped him in the Styx
To make his chance of dying nix;
Alas, the heel she held him by
Remained unfortunately dry.
So look out, boys, for other heels
Who're apt to hand you dirty deals.

AGAMEMNON, GREEK LEGEND, LEADER OF THE GREEK ARMIES IN THE TROJAN WAR

Agamemnon, Atreus' son,
Laid seige to Troy, at long last won,
With help reduced that place to chaos,
Got Helen back for Menelaus.
(Paris, remember, swiped the dame
And brought them both eternal fame,)
Went home to Clytemnestra, wife —
Was greeted by a fatal knife.
So this roaming hero came to an end
In a way he certainly didn't intend.

ALEXANDER THE GREAT,
356-323 B.C. KING OF MACEDON

King and soldier, Alexander
Liked to fight but not philander.
Conquered nations, named a city,
Was queerly mixed of hate and pity;
Won in every war endeavor,
But died at thirty-three of fever.
You'd think an exit should be grander
For a hero like great Alexander —
Ord'nry folks can make a louder
Noise when they take a powder.

ANANIAS AND SAPHIRA, CIRCA 50 A.D. ACTS 5:1-11

To escape the fate of these doomed two,
Be very careful that you do
Not try to cheat the mighty Lord.
They did, and Peter said a word
That knocked them flat as a flower bed,
That is to say, they fell down dead.
So look out then you dames and sires,
That is, all you modern liars.

ANTONY, MARC, 86-30 B.C.
ROMAN POLITICIAN AND SOLDIER

Marcus Antonius, lucky cat,
Was by birth aristocrat;
Became a lot of mighty things
Very little short of kings,
But let us briefly now report
(Just to make the story short)
What he did in special cases:
In Egypt, Rome, and other places.
Say like his eloquent oration
After the base assassination
Of mighty Caesar, the people's friend,
Thus brought to an untimely end.
He very subtly wrought upon
The hostile mob, and one by one
Turned their hearts to Caesar's cause
Minus any hems and haws.
But later, alas, he set up house
(Forsaking thus his lawful spouse)
With Cleopatra, beauteous, glamorous,
And much much more than common amorous.
The outcome of this love-sick folly
Makes a story not very jolly.
He did himself in, thinking Cleo
Had erstwhile gone to meet her Deo,
Just because she'd turned away
And left for home on a naval day.

ASPASIA, 5TH CENTURY B.C.
GREEK COURTESAN

Aspasia was witty,
Aspasia was smart,
Her charm ('twasn't pity)
Won Pericles' heart.
The gents in that era
Eschewed flesh alone,
They chose the haetera
To give their lives tone.
'Spase didn't care
(*Suspect* though this is)
That though learned and fair
She was never made Mrs.

THE HOUSE OF ATREUS
AND AGAMEMNON
GREEK MYTHOLOGY

A gory clan was the House of Atreus,
Their yen for slaughter was infatuous.
The branch by Agamemnon headed
With blood was most especially redded.
He slew Iphigenia, youngest daughter,
To appease the gods of wind and water.
Because of this and his girl friend Cassie
(He met in Troy, the royal lassie)
Spouse Clytemnestra with her lover
Killed this ten-year absent rover
Cassandra too, and nothing grievin'
Gloated that she was even-Steven.
But son Orestes was sore about this,
He figured he could do without this —
That is, the slaughter of his daddie
When he was a small and banished laddie.
Sister Electra too was burning,
To take revenge on Mamma yearning.
So Clytemnestra, could you refute it?
Was Orestes — and Electracuted.

AURELIUS, MARCUS, 121-180 A.D.
ROMAN EMPEROR

Emperor of Rome for a passel of years,
Marcus's reign was not without tears.
Earthquakes and plagues and attacks from without
Required that at all times his heart should be stout.
But despite all catastrophies, terrors, and fights,
He drew some of the teeth of the local tax bites,
That is for the poor for whom his heart bled
Unless they were Christians (or so it is said.)
He favored the Stoics of which he was one,
So to persecute Christians was part of his fun.
He sat down and wrote his book MEDITATIONS,
Which is read to this day by nearly all nations,
And tells with great beauty the ways of the Stoics
Which seem to us moderns a kind of heroics.
We only could wish an Aurelius with axes
Would come along now and chop off our taxes,
Not for the rich or the poor — they never pay any,
But for hardworking dopes that can't save a penny.

BACON, FRANCIS, 1561-1626,
ENGLISH PHILOSOPHER
AND STATESMAN

Francis Bacon hadn't any
Morals when it came to money.
Lord Chancellor for James the First,
He fell for bribes, confessed the worst;
Was fined a pile and sent to prison,
Repented there and was forgiven.
Retired and wrote the learned tomes
Not found in ordinary homes,
But said to revolutionize
The search for knowledge science-wise.

Bath-Sheba was a naughty girl,
She bathed in view of David's roof,
Put his head into a whirl —
His conduct after was the proof.
He courted her with honeyed words
To which the lady soon succumbed —
Hubby was strictly for the birds,
At Uriah the Hittite her nose she thumbed.
David hastened Uriah's demise,
In the front of battle had him placed,
Married the gal despite her size,
Otherwise she'd have been disgraced.
And if this tale shows David not
A virtuous type to think upon,
It must have been a heavenly plot:
Their second son was Solomon.

BELL, ALEXANDER GRAHAM, 1847-1922, AMERICAN SCIENTIST, INVENTOR OF TELEPHONE

If you have stock in Tel and Tel,
Thank Alexander Graham Bell.
And hail while on the party line
The phone he made at twenty-nine.
He fathered mass communication,
The bane of every earthly nation.
The more that people get together,
Stormier and stormier gets the weather.
The pretty dream of Wendell Wilkie
Is as far from here as the Way called Milky.
The more folks know of one another,
To fight like hell is what they'd druther.

BOLEYN, ANNE, 1507-1536,
QUEEN CONSORT OF HENRY VIII

Anne Boleyn was a naughty maid,
She bunked with her lord ere the rites were said,
But Henry made her queen at last
And she thought she'd hooked the fellow fast.
But though she gave the king an heir:
Elizabeth beyond compare,
(Who later ruled with great distinction,
Dooming her rivals to extinction)
Henry's ardor failed most sadly,
No longer did he love her madly.
So to the block he had her led
And there the poor girl lost her head.

BROWN, JOHN, 1800-1859, AMERICAN ABOLITIONIST

John Brown failed in every field
Until he struck for freedom's cause,
For which he strove and wouldn't yield,
Disregarding moral laws.
He helped the Negroes, slave and free
And stirred up strife against their foes,
And folks who were pro-slavery? —
Without a qualm he murdered *those.*
At Harper's Ferry General Lee
Caught the guy and kept him there,
Thus never more, alas, could he
Get out to travel anywhere,
Until at last he went to heaven —
At least as many now deduce —
Unhappily the ticket given
Was routed via hangman's noose.

CAESAR, JULIUS, 102?-44 B.C.
ROMAN STATESMAN AND GENERAL

Julius Caesar, mighty Roman,
Priceless friend, but dangerous foeman;
Warrior, statesman, lover, showman,
Toga'd gent afraid of no man.
He ever dared to do his duty,
Which brought him to his "Et tu, Brute"
And Ides of March when traitors nabbed **him**
And in a dozen places stabbed him.
But why should minor scribblers rave on
When he's grandly done by the Bard of Avon!

CARDIGAN, JAMES THOMAS
BRUDENELL, 1797-1868
BRITISH GENERAL

Cardigan, the 7th Earl of,
Deemed himself a priceless pearl of
British generals, et set.,
(A misconception generals get).
Fancying thus he led his troops
On a dashing charge, not dreaming, oops!
He headed in the wrong direction,
Which gave the stunt a new complexion.
Suddenly surprised, astounded,
By mighty cannon roar surrounded,
Back and front and sideways shot at,
From every angle straightly got at —
Why dwell though on this dreary matter
Resulting in such bloody spatter?
Alas the guy was made immortal
After he'd entered heaven's portal.
Tennyson raised that blundering shade
By writing *The Charge of the Light Brigade,*
A sonorously rolling poem
Without which few would ever know him.
"Cannon to right and left of them
Volleyed and thundered,
Into the Valley of Death
Rode the six hundered."

or

"Cannon to right and left of them
Volleyed and thundred,
Into the Valley of Death
Rode the six hundred."

P.S. This was in Crimea
In case you thought it was Korea,
And it certainly wasn't Tennyson
Who named a sweater for the son-of-a-gun.

CARROL, LEWIS (CHARLES LUTWIDGE DODGSON) 1832-1898 ENGLISH WRITER AND MATHEMATICIAN

Lewis Carrol delighted all,
Even the queen Victoria!
To read him was to have a ball,
Be blessed with sweet euphoria.
That is his ALICE IN WONDERLAND,
A truly ludicrous chronicle,
But hidden in it, contraband,
A meaning quite ironical.
Victoria yearned for more of same
(Not knowing there wasn't any
And that Lewis Carrol wasn't his name)
Thus her eyes most popped out when he
Sent all his works as she commanded:
Solemn tomes on mathematics
(Some would call it underhanded)
Properer for math fanatics,
Charles Lutwidge Dodgson signed
(Far from what she had in mind.)
March Hare, Mad Hatter, Queens White and Red
Were the curious folk she sought instead.

CASSANDRA, GREEK LEGEND, TROJAN PRINCESS

Princess Cassandra, Priam's daughter,
Was done to as it hadn't oughter.
The apple of Apollo's eye,
He taught her how to prophecy,
But when this love-sick god Apollo
Beckened and she would not follow,
He decreed none would believe her,
A curse that did most sorely grieve her;
And then when Agamemnon looted
Conquered Troy, he found she suited
His every taste in girlish beauty
And took her home against his duty
To Clytemnestra, long time spousy,
An act she thought was truly lousy,
And with an eye to her survival
She very promptly slew her rival —
Hubby too as you'll see later,
Her children's most unlucky pater.

CHESTERFIELD, PHILIP DORMER STANHOPE, 4th EARL OF, 1694-1773
ENGLISH STATESMAN, ORATOR, AND AUTHOR

Although his Lordship's morals were lax,
"Don't follow in your poppa's tracks"
Was not advice he gave his son,
Philip Stanhope, bastard one.
He wrote instead a batch of letters
Telling him how to ape his betters
In everything but sex relations
On which he made no dissertations.

CIRCE, GREEK LEGEND,
CELEBRATED ENCHANTRESS

If one should ask you, "Who is Circe?"
The answer is Belle Dame Sans Merci.
She hexed the luckless shipwrecked strangers
Upon an island fraught with dangers,
Kept their wits alive and fine
But turned their bodies into swine.
But great Ulysses after Troy-ing
And homeward bound found it annoying
To see his brave and loyal crewman
Converted thus to nothing human.
"You can't do this to me," he shouted,
But Hermes (god) this something doubted
And gave the guy a magic potion
To render true this pleasing notion.
Circe was at first affrighted
And then most perfectly delighted.
With out-stretched arms she said, "Odysseus,
What do you say to a little Kiss-eous?"
"Why not," he thought, I fail to see
The rush to join Penelope."
'Twas thus some years before (a-slowing)
He said, "I really must be going."
He took off then and found his wife
Leading a dull but virtuous life.

COLETTE, 1873-1954
FRENCH NOVELIST

Colette wrote fascinating works
About the ladies and their quirks.
She had uncanny knowledge of
The way they acted when in love —
And that was, girlies, all the time
From early morn 'til midnight chime.
And some had fancies rather queer,
Like courting one another, dear.
But most of them we're glad to say
Loved gents in quite a normal way.
Eroticism she showed in full,
Never did she punches pull,
But this sans those four-letter terms
So popular with sexy worms.

CROESUS Died circa 546 B.C.
KING OF LYDIA

Croesus conquered Ionian cities
But was friendly to the losers
(Maybe he sang some victory ditties
And joined hilarious boozers.)
But when affrighted by Persia's Cyrus,
(With Egypt and Babylonia)
He fought him and died of battle virus
(It could've been pneumonia.)
But to be as rich as Croesus
We'd welcome such come-uppance,
Indeed 'twould very greatly please us
Who haven't got a tuppence.

DAEDALUS, GREEK MYTHOLOGY
SCULPTOR AND ARTIST

Daedalus, in Greek Mythol,
Artist, architect, withal,
Built for Minos, king of Crete
A labyrinth marvelously neat
In which to put the Minotaur,
His exit perfectly to bar.
This monster, hideous and horrid,
Was born to Mrs. Minos (torrid!)
It seems she fell for a lot of bull,
 Which certainly wasn't dutiful.
Ungrateful Minos locked Daedalus **up,**
Icarus too, the fellow's pup —
So Papa made them each a pair
Of waxen wings to fly from there,
Warning the boy to not go near
The Sun or he'd melt and disappear.
But do you think that lad would **heed**
His Daddy's warning? No indeed.
He soared and soared ever higher
And was consumed by old Sol's fire.
May we suggest that fathers are not
As dumb as sons assume them, what?

DAMOCLES, SYRACUSAN
AT COURT OF DIONYSIUS

Damocles was Dionysius's stooge,
A truly nauseating sycophant,
So Dion, disapproving, forthwith sought
To give this silly man a different slant.
He made a sumptuous banquet for the guy,
Which seemed to Damocles the very most,
'Til looking up he spied a glittering sword
Hung high above — by order of his host.
Suspended by a single hair it hung,
And like to fall at any given minute —
'Twas thus he learned that every high estate
Had much of woe and much of danger in it.
Today, alas, the Sword of Damocles
Does not confine itself to ruling folk,
It hangs above the heads of working stiffs,
That is to say we're all kept stony broke
By every kind of tax man e'er devised,
In danger too of freeways, planes, et cet,
Air pollution, water ditto, so
Damo's fix seems now a minor threat.

DANTE ALIGHIERI, 1266-1321,
ITALIAN POET

You've heard of Dante's INFERNO,
He also wrote as if there were no
Pesky sex to mar man's dreaming
And urge him on to acts unseeming,
That is, in re his Beatrice,
Lovelier than any modern miss,
His love for her was pure and holy
Albeit something melancholy.
Alas, he had another nature
(You know of course its nomenclature)
And this persuaded him to marry,
The which he did, and not to tarry.
Thus without an ounce of trouble
He led a perfect life — but double,
But if not to social rules complaint,
A famous literary giant:
His COMEDY, divine but horrible
Pictured MAN as quite incorrigible,
Which sends him to the hellish regions
Where live the damned by many legions.

DAPHNE, GREEK MYTHOLOGY

Daphne was the oddest of lasses,
She didn't relish masculine passes
Though plentiful (she didn't wear glasses)
She was adored by handsome Apollo,
Thither and yon he did her follow
Everywhere o'er hill and hollow.
The naughty god continued to chase her
Praying very soon to face her
And at last in joy embrace her.
But very soon he came to see
This marvel was not meant to be:
She prayed and was changed to a laurel tree!
Now laurel trees are very nice
But as mates do not at all suffice,
Ask any human male — no dice!

DEMOSTENES, 384?-122 B.C.
GREATEST OF GREEK ORATORS

Demosthenes was a bitter foe
Of Philip of Macedon,
He delivered many an oral blow
At him and his famous son.
But despite his golden eloquence
In PHILLIPICS 1, 2, 3,
The dark and gloomy consequence
Came increasingly to be
That Philip dominated Greece:
(In warring, old and young
Find swords for fighting *pere* or *fils*
Mightier than the tongue.)
That story, incidentally
Re cramming his mouth with rocks
And shouting at the roaring sea
Is due for a couple of socks.
In other words, it's but a fib,
Spicier than the truth —
It's always jollier to *ad lib*
Than stick to the facts, forsooth.

DIOGENES, c. 412-323 B.C., GREEK CYNIC PHILOSOPHER

"The virtuous life is the simple life —"
So said Diogenes;
He lived in a tub but not to wash:
Encouraging flies and fleas.
Daytime he carried a lantern about,
Looking for a *man,*
Showing he took a very dim view
Of his fellows — not their fan.
Without a doubt he was Hippie the First,
Long on hair and varied dirts
And could've done as noses found
With a ton of BAN and CERTS.

DOYLE, SIR ARTHUR CONAN,
1859-1930, ENGLISH AUTHOR

Hail to Arthur Conan Doyle,
Born on Scotland's northern soil,
Doctor Doyle he first became,
Successfully eluding fame.
Gave up dosing, settled down
To write, and fabulous renown,
And though subsequently knighted
For patriotic tracts indited
It was indeed that super-sleuth
Art invented in his youth:
Sherlock Holmes (whose vast acumen
Exceeded that of any human)
Who brought the world to Arthur's feet,
Considering it a precious treat
To sit up nights and lose their sleep
To see that Moriarity-creep
Get from Holmes a swift come-uppance
Easy to Holmes as the flip of a tuppence;
And laugh at Dr. Watson's grumbling
Along with his endearing mumbling
But late in life Doyle got to prying
In things that happened after dying,
Hocus-pocus often hosting
As he blithely went a-ghosting.

DRAKE, SIR FRANCIS, 1540-1596, ENGLISH NAVIGATOR AND ADMIRAL

At a tender age Drake took to sea
And early proved efficiency,
But 'twarn't 'till 1572
That he really showed what he could do.
With 74 men and but two ships,
He made his first marauding trips;
Took towns, burned ships, and copped trains three
With thirty tons of silver, whee!
Later Good Queen Bess said, "Drake,
Go and Spanish holdings take
'Way away on the Pacific Coast,
But keep it dark that I'm your host."
So Francis did, and thus he found
Treasure beyond two million pound,
Which pleased Elizabeth no end,
But lost Spain's Philip as a friend.
Such conniving fooled him not at all,
So Elizabeth said, "To hell with y'all"
And knighted Francis straight away,
Which doubtless made him shout "Hooray!"
Vice Admiral of the English fleet
He gained a victory very sweet;
Brought the Spanish Armada down,
Though some of the Spainards stuck around.

ELEANOR OF ACQUITAINE
1122-1204, QUEEN OF HENRY II OF ENGLAND (And BORGIA, LUCRETIA 1480-1519, FAMOUS FIGURE OF THE ITALIAN RENAISSANCE

Eleanor 'n Lucretia were famous gals
(Unlike Cathy of Russia they married their pals)
Lucretia by gossip was grossly maligned,
Eleanor by Henry was long time confined.
Actually Lou was an amiable kind.
Eleanor seemed partial to high-ranking Hals,
Lou wed Alphonsos at short intervals.
Nell wived and mothered several kings,
Dick Coeur de Lion her son of all things!
The two of them sponsored both letters and art,
Their courts they made places delighting the heart;
And Lou didn't poison as foul legend sings,
Nor Nell murder Rosy despite hubby's flings.

FRANKLIN, BENJAMIN, 1706-1790
AMERICAN STATESMAN, PRINTER,
SCIENTIST, AND WRITER

Some say Mrs. F. in a moment of strife —
Not being a very conforming wife —
Said to her spouse, "I loathe this fight,
So kindly scram and fly a kite."
He flew a kite all right all right,
But for another reason quite.
So read about it, lazy boneses,
Be smarter than the Smiths and Joneses.
Read how he won a great renown
In parts removed from his home town;
What he did at home one day
And where he went for the U.S.A.
Remember that famous Declaration
Denouncing British occupation?

GALATEA — GREEK MYTHOLOGY

Pygmalion sculped a female form
From marble cold and lifeless,
So beautiful he sorrowed that
It made him thenceforth wifeless.
But while he doted in despair,
He prayed to Aphrodite
Who turned the statute into flesh —
Made everything alrighty —
A circumstance that GBS
And all his future heirs
Had no reason to deplore:
It made them millionaires.

GENGHIS KAHN, 1167-1227, MONGOL CONQUEROR

Genghis Kahn was a gory guy,
He slaughtered without ruth,
Sparing nothing in his path,
In a manner most uncouth.
He conquered many countries, pals,
With names too hard to spell,
Raided Persia and what is now
South Russia, gave 'em hell.
But withal a brilliant ruler,
Or so 'tis widely said,
Still anyone who crosed his path
Needed a prompt exam of his head.

EL GRECO, 1541-1614,
GREEK PAINTER IN SPAIN

El Greco, the Greek
With a name unpronounceable,
Moved early to Spain
For a career undenounceable.
He painted the nobles
Of the city Toledo —
(Those were the days
Before tails or tuxedo)
But oddly his subjects
Had such extra long limbs,
Arms, necks and torsos,
That in singing their hymns
How the parts got together
For a musical tone
Is something to ponder
And really unknown.
One wonders and wonders
Without ifs or buts
At the miles upon, miles upon,
Miles upon guts.

GWYNNE, ELEANOR, 1650-1687, ENGLISH ACTRESS

A time there was when a girl like Nell
Was said to be en route to hell,
But judged by female doings now
She wore a halo on her brow.
This sprightly maiden started out
Selling fruit to gent and lout,
Beside the Theatre Royal door,
But soon was seller, maid, no more.
Became an actress playing parts
That captured many manly hearts,
But most enthusiastically reckoned
The cat's meow by Charles the Second.
But why say more except to add
A brace of boys this couple had
Without the benefit of minister,
Marking them with the bar called sinister.

HADRIAN, A.D. 76-138,
ROMAN EMPEROR

Hadrian, Emperor of Rome,
Did wonders abroad as well as at home,
He interspersed his splendid rule
(Not often read about in school)
With building long and mighty walls,
The sight of which the eye enthralls.
Great Britain's is the masterpiece,
Praise of it will never cease;
But further walls of great renown
Are seen in many a foreign town.
As to the Emperor's private life —
Well it's true he took a wife,
But what about that handsome youth
Whose face and form he caused forsooth
(And what folks thought he didn't care)
To be in statues everywhere?
It seems that in those early days
Boys loved boys in torrid ways,
So no one made a bit of fuss
About his favorite, Antinous.

HELEN OF TROY GREEK LEGEND, DAUGHTER OF ZEUS AND LEDA

You won't believe it: beauteous Helen,
The most delightful luscious melon,
Wasn't born in the regular way,
At least that's what the legends say.
Her pa, that mighty god called Zeus,
To procreate had little use
For usual ordinary means,
He had another way with queens.
He courted Leda as a swan,
And so she laid an egg — Go-wan!
And hatched, that goddess did, a girl,
Gorgeous Helen, priceless pearl.
Helen grew and lovelier waxed,
So Grecian nobles weren't relaxed
Once they clapped their eyes upon her,
But Menelaus finally won her.
Menelaus, King of Sparta,
Thereafter soon became a martyr.
For Paris, son of Troy's Priam,
Said to himself, "fellow I am
A-going to swipe that luscious prize,
Cut Menelaus down to size."
So he did, and thus Le Roy
Soon engaged in war with Troy,
Along with Agamemnon, brother,
And friends and nobles many another.
They formed a fleet and sailed to Troy

("Hello there, and ship ahoy!")
Gave Helen the joys if not the rights
Of lazy days and lively nights.
For ten long years Spartans besieged
That city of Troy, so bravely leiged,
Till finally the Trojans tired,
The last bit of their poop expired.
"All right, all right," they were moved to say,
"Take the gal, a curse to men,
And darken not our shores again."
And Menelaus, pleased or not?
He sadly thought of the fun he'd got
In all that time without his melon,
Gorgeous and delightful Helen.
But there it was and so he brought her
Home, and later had a daughter,
But of all the years that lay ahead
The less the better may be said.
He got cranky, she got scrawny,
And all their days were dully yawny.

HOMER, ANCIENT GREEK
LITERARY FIGURE

Scholars (?) hated to admit it,
But in Seven Hundred, about, B.C.,
The poet Homer lived and wrote
THE ILLIAD and the ODYSSEY.
This bugs them like the seven-year itch,
(Their kind is always taking
The credit away from men of fame
And assiduously a-making
The charge that others did their stuff —
Bacon Shakespeare's plays for instance —
It lets them feel they're not as dumb
As they appear from any distance.)
But here's to Homer, without whom
We'd not have met the peerless Helen,
And learned about the seige of Troy
So thrilling in the poet's tellin'.
Nor heard about the ten-year trip
Homeward of the great Ulysses,
Suggesting he was not too keen
To see Penelope, his missus.

IBSEN, HENRIK, 1829-1906,
NORWEGIAN POET AND DRAMATIST

Henrik Ibsen was among the first
To grant that every female
Was more than slave — indeed he durst
Declare she should have the rights of a he-male.
He did this in his DOLL'S HOUSE play,
And all gals should salute him,
Though guys up to this very day
Do their damnedest to refute him.

JACKSON, THOMAS JONATHAN
(STONEWALL) 1824-1863,
CONFEDERATE GENERAL

Bull Run was the name of the game
Where Jackson got his sobriquet;
As General Barnard Bee declared,
"He stood like a stone wall" in the fray.
Next to General Robert E. Lee
The army loved Stonewall the most,
And so it was a bitter blow
When very early he was lost.
Killed in the darkness by his own,
One of war's sad accidents,
That left the army desolate,
And greatly weakened in defense.
Stonewall was a pious man
With many quaint and curious quirks
Which made him of more interest
Than dull and ordinary jerks.

JAEL, BIBLICAL HEROINE,
JUDGES 4:5 ET. SEQ

Jael had a way with her
That led Sisera to stay with her
As sanctuary from his foes —
Her husband's friend, the saying goes.
She hammered nails into his head
Until he was completely dead.
So generals nowadays best flee
Some ladies' hospitality.

JEFFERSON, THOMAS, 1743-1826
THIRD PRESIDENT OF
THE UNITED STATES

Everybody, everywhere
Knows Thomas Jefferson wrote
The Declaration of Independence which
Is a document of note.
They know he was a governor,
Pres, and all that there,
Scientist and architect
With talents sans compare.
But all folks think of when they think
At all about the man
Are his remarks in that famed piece
With supposedly dead pan.
He didn't mean them that's for sure,
For no one but a fool
Would think that all were equal born
Though you heard he did, in school.
The equality he wrote about
Was strictly under law —
He'd turn smack over in his grave
At conclusions folks now draw.
He'd side with Alex Hamilton
Instead of present nuts
Who claim all people are the same
With equal brains and guts.

JOHNSON, SAMUEL, 1709-1794,
ENGLISH AUTHOR

Like the poet Keats, Sam's antecedents
Weren't earls or kings or even regents.
His pater though an honest feller
Was nothing but a poor bookseller.
And Sam himself, a brilliant scholar,
Chased in vain the elusive dollar.
And besides not being wealthy
This poor guy wasn't even healthy.
He was also quite a seether,
Not known for grace or beauty either.
But yet a conversationalist
Whose wit and charm few could resist.
He also did a lot of writing
Not all of which was found inviting,
Alas it sparkled with invective
Some thought offensively corrective.
But that which brought his reputation
Miles above its former station:
A mammoth tome, a dictionary,
Marvelously literary,
But giving very comic meanings
To match his own eccentric leanings.
But none of this would have been his doing
Without that rare old cultured bird,
Damned in America, George the Third.

JUDITH, THE APOCRYPHA
(Circa 100 B.C.)

When Holophernes attacked the Jews
On Judith he didn't reckon.
Too late alas he learned the news
That this beauty had only to beckon
And he would follow like a lamb
And get himself into a jam.
Beware, then, every snooty warrior
The beckoning maid, or you'll be sorrier.

KEY, FRANCIS SCOTT,
1779-1843, AMERICAN POET,
U.S. ATTORNEY FOR DISTRICT
OF COLUMBIA

THE STAR SPANGLED BANNER, wrote F. S.
  Key,
A patriotic lyric,
But very few can reach high C —
And it all sounds a bit hysteric
But all its sentiments we commend
And intend to sing it world without end.

KHAYYAM, OMAR, ELEVENTH CENTURY, PERSIAN POET AND MATHEMATICIAN

"Ah, my computations, people way
Reduce the year to better reckoning — Nay
'Twas only striking from the calendar
Unborn tomorrow and dead yesterday."
So in modesty the poet spoke
Of the great reform in Time a group of folk
Of scientific talent worked upon
Beyond the powers of any common bloke.
But all that, dears, is just about forgot,
So charmed are we with Omar's RUBAIYAT,
Exhorting us to steep ourselves in wine —
That pagan argument that God is not
But this is wicked heresy we know,
Lovely in form but thankfully not so.
Our thanks to poet Ed Firzgerald too
Whose version made those quatrains lovelier grow.
Thus let us, friends, take with a grain of salt
Omar's counsel re the Grape, and halt
Our imbibations of its fermented juice
And reach with grim reluctance for a malt.

LAFAYETTE, MARIE JOSEPH
PAUL YVES ROCH GILBERT
DU MOTIER MARQUISE de,
1757-1834, FRENCH STATESMAN
AND SOLDIER

This nobleman of many names
Was fond of revolutions:
He thought they were delightful games
For problems' diminutions.
Now some may think that point is moot
And harbor views quite other,
Regarding it a crime to shoot,
And everyone each one's brother.
But let us thank our lucky stars
The Marquise's disposition
Was rather on the side of wars,
A boon to our condition.
He sailed the seas to fight with us
Against invading British,
And never showed in all that fuss
A sign of being skittish.

LINCOLN, ABRAHAM, 1809-1865, 16th PRESIDENT OF THE UNITED STATES

Honest Abe was born in a cabin
But decided to move to the White House,
And so to guide his people right,
Make it a sort of lighthouse.
He didn't go to school at all,
Not having enough of pelf,
But being an ambitious lad,
He went and taught himself.
And though his learning was enough
For the President of our nation,
They wouldn't give him a job today
Selling gas at a service station.
If you'd know all about the wonderful guy,
Sandburg's is the book to buy.

MAINTENON, FRANCOISE
D'AUBIGNE, MARQUISE de,
1635 - 1719

Francoise was a lovely frail
Despite the fact she was born in jail,
Because her poppa had betrayed
The Protestant cause, or so 'twas said.
But soon she wed Scarron, the poet,
Became a lit'ry dame — you'd know it!
But then he croaked, so she got a post
With Madame Montespan, the most
In Louis Fourteenth's gay affections,
(Monarchs had such predilections!).
All that Francie was hired to do
Was teach the kids, but she slyly drew
Louis' love and soft attention
(In ways we can't politely mention,)
From Montespan to Widow Scarron,
Hardly of virtue a seeming paragon.
Marie Theresa, the really queen,
Adored her too, as plainly seen,
And in her rival's strong embrace
Breathed her last, a very odd place
You'll admit in the circumstances,
Though her tale it thus enhances,
And proves that sirens like Francoise
Are murder to both girls and boys.

MARY, QUEEN OF SCOTLAND,
1542 - 1587

Mary, Mary, Queen of Scots,
A gal of charm and beauty,
Hatched some pretty spicy plots
Not in the line of duty.
'Twas said she murdered Darnley, spouse,
Or had her Bothwell do it,
Blowing up the poor guy's house,
Strangling him when he flew it.
She longed to be great England's queen,
And thought she had a right to,
Indeed was quite prepared, 'twas seen,
To finagle and to fight to.
So naturally the Good Queen Bess,
A monarch strong and mighty,
Took to this notion less and less,
And thought it pretty flighty.
And so anon it came to pass
Poor Mary was beheaded,
A fate that she had long, alas,
Most passionately dreaded.
But she had courage, she had brains,
In spite of dereliction —
She had a lot more joys and pains
Than heroines of fiction.

MIDAS, GREEK LEGEND,
8TH CENTURY B.C.
KING OF PHRYGIA

Somehow, they say, our Midas won
Dionysius's favor,
Was given the power to turn to gold
All he touched, sans flavor,
A circumstance he found to be
Decidedly unhandy —
The staunchest stomach can't digest
Golden meat or candy.
But Dionysius made him lave
In small Pactolus river
Whose waters washed away that gift,
Delighting Midas' liver.
King of Phrygia was he
BC about Eight Hundred,
And Getty-like he piled up dough
While lesser folks were plundered.
He was also first to bring an end
To inconvenient barter,
By making coins to swap for stuff:
And he never was a martyr.

NELSON, HORATIO 1758-1805
ENGLISH NAVAL HERO

Viscount Nelson, i.e. Horatio
Was a famous English naval hero.
His preacher poppa would have thought
He did some things he hadn't ought
Though proud he surely would have been
If he had known, if he had seen
Horatio's exploits in the wars,
The pastimes of the mighty Mars.
He lost an eye and then an arm
But never viewed with much alarm;
Won battles here and battles there
With skill and valor past compare,
But fell like bricks for Sir Hamilton's lady,
Which led to doings something shady.
And here's a fact that will astound you,
If not most utterly confound you:
He went to live with her and her lord,
Actually he did, *my word!*
But never did this odd arrangement
(You'd think that he'd prefer estrangement)
Reflect on Cape Trafalgar, rather
There he worked himself into a lather,
Destroyed the fleets both French and Spanish,
Feats fatal but also super-mannish.

NERO, CLAUDIUS CAESAR, A.D.
37-68, ROMAN EMPEROR

Nero was a matricide,
An uxorcide twice over,
In fact just every king of-cide
The murderous can discover.
He wanted to recite a piece
Anent famed Troy's falling,
So set a raging fire in Rome
To make it more appalling.
He went to the Olympic games and won
In poetry competitions —
For who would dare to risk his head
Through victory in such conditions?
He never ceased to seek the fun
He got from reckless slaying;
Right and left he slashed and slew
As if he went a-Maying.
But Seneca and the Praetorian guard
Soon joined the hostile forces,
The jig was up so he slew himself
To escape a fate that worse is —
Such as his murdered mistress-wife,
A dame y-clept Poppaea,
Would've wished to see befall the beast
Sans a single *culpa mea*.

NEWTON, SIR ISAAC, 1642-1727
ENGLISH SCIENTIST

Sir Isaac said so far he saw
(He discovered gravitation's law
Watching an apple fall to ground —
The principle of which he did expound)
Because he stood on giants' shoulders,
And together they became the moulders
Of many scientific rules
Taught afterward in science schools:
Broke white light into colors, then
Converted them to white again;
Great mathematician, physicist
Whose fame forever will exist,
Though true the ordinary guy
Seldom asks the reason why,
Content to know that apples fall
And conk you on the bean, that's all.

OCTAVIA, d 11 B.C., WIFE OF MARC ANTONY, (SISTER OF ROMAN EMPEROR AGUSTUS)

Octavia was an unusual dame,
The world has known but few of same;
Beautiful and virtuous too —
A combination hard to brew.
She may have wept but she didn't scold
When her Antony had made so bold
As to cast her off for a siren's sake —
Cleopatra was on the make.
And when these lovers were deceased
(The population they'd increased)
She took their progeny to raise,
And Fulvia's too, the record says.
Add these to Antony's and hers
And you have a bunch of saboteurs
Of peace and quiet in the home
Enough to make most mothers roam.
The moral of this tale is that
A gentleman who loves to cat
Should marry first a lady who
Will keep the kids when he's dead of woo.

PARKER, DOROTHY ROCHSCHILD, 1893-1967, AMERICAN SHORT STORY AND VERSE WRITER

Dorothy Parker knew all about love,
Its pitfalls and its dangers;
Its perils she held far above
The threats of savage strangers.
"Eschew l'amour" was her advice,
"Dodge slyly cupid's darts,
Be virtuous and ever nice,
Keep yours the Whole-of-Hearts,
But if your life's not worth a damn
Do not blame *me*, my little lamb!"

PETRONIUS B.C. 66,
ROMAN SATIRIST

Patronius Arbiter lived it up
But in such an elegant style
Nero made him plan *his* fetes
His boredom to beguile.
Profligate and indolent
Were the words applied to Pete,
But as pro— and consul to Bythinia
And writer he was neat.
But he incurred the jealousy
Of one Tigellinus
Who wished his spot in Nero's court
That seemed so marvelous
But when Petronius' doom appeared
To be quite imminent
Petronius foiled the villian's plan
And covetous intent.
Putting on a party such
As few had ever seen
Surrounded too by all his pals
And a gal like to a queen,
He opened his patrician veins
And let the blue blood flow,
And when the fun was at its height,
Petronius was no mo'.

POITER, DIANE de, 1499-1566
DUCHESS OF VALENTINOUS

Henry the Second chose to play
With charming Diane de Poitier;
Wife Cathy de Medici favored her too
(Queens go along when their husbands woo —
Not that they would if they had a choice
But they seldom have a deciding voice.)
Diane also played it cool,
The gal was aught but anyone's fool.
In diplomatic circles where
Fortunes change (like the color hair,
That is today) and whatever power
Was topmost at a given hour,
Montmorency be it or Guise,
She was agin it, deeming it wise.
Alas her kingly paramour
Succumed at last to heaven's lure
And she was forced to leave the court
Where prudery had small support;
But while it lasted it was grand
Exclamation! Ampersand!

POMPADOUR, JEANNE ANTOINETTE POISSON LE NORMANT D'ETOILLES, MARQUISE de, 1721-1764
FRENCH BEAUTY

This charming lady with a lot of names
(As if she were one of the high-born dames)
Stole the heart of Louis Fifteen,
Who made her his mistress, not his queen.
She wrested the sceptre from his hand
And ruled la France; at her command
This and that and t'other were done,
Plus fortunes spent on every one
Of all her many residences —
Surrounded, dears, by walls or fences —
Which made the people truly hate her
Since hers was not a royal pater.
But beautiful and smart and witty,
They couldn't stop her from sitting pretty;
Louis Quinze was too betwitched
To have this dazzling siren ditched.

PYTHAGORAS, c 582-507 B.C., GREEK PHILOSOPHER

Pythagoras founded a brotherhood,
Aristotle knew about,
Though evidently not acquainted with
The man himself, at least there's doubt.
But the story goes Pythagoras
Thought numbers could express the whole
Of all that's in the universe:
To prove it was his constant goal.
But whether this he did or not,
There's one thing we can know for sure:
Pounding the theory into kids
Brings them a blessing they abjure.

QUEENSBERRY, JOHN SHOLTO DOUGLAS, THE MARQUESS OF, 1844-1900, ENGLISH NOBLEMAN

Marquess of Queensberry, J. S. D.,
Drafted the rules for BOXING,
So stubbornly resolved was he
To end all prize-ring foxing.
And thus by Eighteen Eighty-nine
His code has been accepted
In England and the U.S.A
And up to now they've kept it.
But in his private life it seems
He faced a bit of scandal,
His son Lord Alfred had a friend
Sticky a bit to handle.
The fellow's name was Oscar Wilde,
And Pa wrote Wilde a letter —
A public one insulting him
(Really he should have known better.)
Wilde sued but dropped the useless suit —
Alas for damning rumors,
Which added to Queensberry's cause
Brought on convicting humors.

RASPUTIN, GREGORI, 1872-1916, RUSSIAN MONK NOTORIOUS FIGURE AT COURT OF NICHOLAS II

Rasputin was a crafty boy
Who made the Russian Tsar his toy,
Starting first with Nicholas's lady
Who wouldn't believe the guy was shady.
He had a fatal magnetism
That brought about a family schism
Though well it worked for the Tsarevich
Curing his hemophilia which
Was wont to take a person off
Be he slave or be he toff.
Though Russian patriots got cranky
They couldn't stop his hanky-panky.
He and the lady ruled the Tsar
And connived with Germans in the war.
Finally enemies fed him poison
Enough to kill a baker's dozen,
But this monster man wasn't even phased.
At last the mob, now really crazed
Attacked this devil's spawn en masse,
Causing his end to come to pass,
A good thing too — this phony monk
Had the odor of a skunk.

RECAMIER, JULIETTE, 1777-1849,
FRENCH BEAUTY
AND SOCIAL FIGURE

Unlike that other Juliette,
This beauty wed platonically —
A banker two times twice her age
But not at all ironically.
Politicos and literateurs
Her salon with pride attending,
Lost their heart in vain to her
Past all hope of mending.
The lady had no use for passion
Although 'twas very much the fashion.

MRS. SOCRATES,
WIFE OF SOCRATES,
GREEK PHILOSOPHER
468-399 B.C.

Xantippe was not known to fame
As a charming and delightful dame.
They say she led her lord a life
Most unbecoming in a wife.
Imagine! she was even irked
Because the fellow never worked,
But went yak-yaking day and night
To set the youths of Athens right.
And doubtless she suppressed a laugh
When Socrates was made to quaff
A spot of hemlock, lethal dose, —
A widow should be lachrymose.

Gertrude started out to be
A real accredited M. D.
But switched to quite another line
Which was for patients' organs fine.
"A rose is a rose is a rose", all right,
But a heart is a heart is a heart we'd fight,
While she was doing this quaint repeat
That poor old pump would cease to beat.
So it's just as well she hied to France
With Toklas, though *she* wore the pants,
Where hopefuls in a writing way
Came chez Stein both night and day
To laugh at her peculiar view
And get for free a meal or two.
But of all the stuff that Gertrude penned
There's little one can recommend.
As far as fame that's lasting goes,
Hers is "a rose is a rose is a rose."

TCHAIKOWSKY, PIOTR ILLICH,
1840-1893 RUSSIAN COMPOSER

If it hadn't been for Madame von Meck,
Who gave him a large annuity,
Concerto in B Flat Minor, we spec
Might never have known futurity.
'Twould have stopped within Tchaikowsky's head
And died, alas, when he did,
Plus all the tunes his genius bred
Were it not for the good that *she* did.
He never met his lady friend,
But they corresponded often:
His fancy took an off-beat trend
His indifferent heart to soften.
But whether you are something queer —
A bit of peculiar-funny,
Genius or nothing anywhere near,
It's nice to be given money.
And it doesn't matter a blank-blank bit
If you never meet who's sending it.

TERMAGANT, MOHAMMEDAN DIETY, REPRESENTED IN ANCIENT MORALITIES AND FARCES

Vociferous, tumultuous and overbearing,
A truly difficult god,
Evidently not a dammit caring
For humans made of sod.
But human males refuted
The thought they were like this jerk
And declare his traits much better suited
To females who went berserk.
So woman is now the termagant,
According to the ego of man,
When she decides to scream and rant
And slap him down, as she can.

UTRILLO, MAURICE,
1883-FRENCH PAINTER

Maurice was the bastard son
Of painter Susanne Valadon,
But writer Miguel Utrillo
Overlooked this pecadillo
On Susanne's part and gave the boy
His legal name, and also joy
(Or at least one would suppose
Though no one that we know of knows)
For Maurice was his mother's son
And painted pictures, every one
Replicas of a well known beat,
That is to say, a Paris street.
Montmartre is the one that's known to all,
And hangs on almost every wall —
Only those are hep to art
Who own a Woolworth of *Montmartre*.

VALENTINE, SAINT,
d. 270 A.D. ROMAN MARTYR-PRIEST

This will shock you but it's true,
Valentine had naught to do
With the day that bears his name —
That derived from pagan fame,
A festival on the fourteenth day
Of February (not June or May)
And how this mix-up came to be
Is mystery still to thee and me.
But it does seem queer a martyr — priest
Hardly a lover to say the least,
Should be held accountable
For problems insurmountable.
For even if your love loves back
Who knows when you will get the sack.

VALENTINO, RUDOLPH, 1895-1926,
AMERICAN MOVING PICTURE ACTOR

Ecstacy and sigh and swoon,
Murmuring airs and *Claire de Lune*
Fervor unsurpassed in man
Plus a most alluring pan.
Of such was Valentino made
Judging by the long parade
Of females who desired to be
Beloved of this gorgeous he,
Supposing when they saw *The Sheik*
And other movies at his peak,
His kiss would scorch a lady love
The way that they'd been dreaming of.
Alas, this handsome ball of fire,
Did not return their keen desire —
He didn't stay to live it up
But at thirty-one turned down the cup,
Dead of a germ that the butcher or
The baker might have fallen for.

WELLS, HERBERT GEORGE, 1866-1946, ENGLISH JOURNALIST AND NOVELIST

H. G. had a squeaky voice
Which didn't make the ear rejoice,
And anything *but* was his English pan
That of a gorgeous handsome man.
Nevertheless he had a mind
You really very seldom find,
So it made no dif, to put it so,
That his beauty score was rather low.
The science fiction tales were great
That emanated from his pate,
His novels of contem'r'ry life
Are with satire and with humor rife.
He wrote *Outline of History*
Which readeth not like a mystery.
And mostly critics are wont to say
About the facts he leads astray,
But if you know any history book
Which doesn't do we'd admire to look.

WHITNEY, ELI, 1765-1825
AMERICAN INVENTOR

Eli Whitney went down south
In seventeen hundred ninety-three,
Studied cotton, and shut my mouth,
Invented the gin immediately.

XERXES, d. 465 B.C.
KING OF PERSIA

Xerxes One, mighty Persian king
(His Bible name Ahaseurus)
Brought Egypt under Persian rule
Which sparked a powerful impetus
To ditto this in Athens, Greece,
(Where else would Athens be you ask us);
Through the Isthmus of Athos a canal he cut
Did this resourceful Ahaseurus.
And over the famous Hellespont,
He made a bridge to cross on,
An idea sans a precedent
(Like rolling stones gathering moss on.)
At Thermopylae Xerxes defeated.
Gen. Leonidas' three hundred Spartans,
But with such advantage over the foe,
Victory was just a wart-man's.
To bring this tale to its doleful end,
His luck petered out at Salamis;
His fleet destroyed, he fled but fast,
"To Asia, for there the balm is."
Alas, it didn't so transpire,
His bodyguard turned traitor,
And slew his boss, quite glad to say,
"So long, old alligator!"

ZEUS. IN GREEK MYTHOLOGY
THE SUPREME GOD

Titan Cronus, Zeus's Dad
Cannibalistic leanings had,
So Mother Rhea son must hide
To keep him out of pa's inside.
Grown up he led victorious war
On Cronus scoring under par;
Then along with brothers two
Divided the universe sans ado.
Poisedon got the turbulent sea
And Hades the underworld, did he,
Leaving Zeus both Heaven and Earth,
The portions of the greatest worth.
Now Zeus kept marrying right and left,
Of wives he never was bereft,
Godesses among them by the score,
And fathered many a goddess more.
Athena sprang from his head full grown,
Aphrodite, Apollo, were his own,
And many another this great god sired,
Of procreating he never tired.
In fact he was in all supreme,
Of all the gods the very cream.
Disobedience he never spared —
Ask Prometheus how *he* fared!